VIVIAN RUSSELL
GNOMES

VIVIAN RUSSELL

GNOMES

FRANCES LINCOLN

PREFACE

A few years ago, after a merry lunch, I bought a set of gnomes and a toadstool as a joke present for my ex-husband, who was all fired up with some grandiose scheme for his cottage garden. The next morning, remembering that the gnome I'd commissioned in his likeness when we were married hadn't been thought very flattering, I had second thoughts. So the gnomes remained in their carrier bag for several months until Annie, the very young daughter of a friend of mine, came for tea. Before she arrived, to entertain her, I lined the gnomes up in the conservatory border, half-hidden in foliage. She really did squeal with delight when she saw them and, from then on, the first thing she'd ask when she came through the door was 'Can I see the gnomes?' I used her visits as an excuse for keeping them there, but to be honest, I was growing fond of the little fellows. It wasn't the lead statue of the exquisite angel delicately poised on his stone plinth that caught my eye every time I passed, but that row of perky red hats, pert noses and cheery faces. There they stood, sturdy boots stuck in the soil, ready to lend a hand. One was leaning on his spade, another proffered a watering can, the third held a pot of flowers. I welcomed them as the new mascots of a garden already made fanciful by topiary birds, rabbits and hens.

Their arrival was like a breath of fresh air. I liked having them around and they were such a novelty that I couldn't stop looking at them. What they brought to my garden was a sense of the ridiculous, which, together with humour, is one of life's best levellers. Italian Renaissance gardens were full of water jokes, *putti* and statues of dwarves. The Greeks painted their statues of gods in bright colours and no one thought them garish. Why have we now become so stuffy and serious, so afraid of the kitsch and the quirky?

During my travels, I searched for new gnomes to add to my collection, stopping off at garden centres around the country. Traditional gnomes were almost nowhere to be found, only an execrable array of crudely produced ornaments. What struck me, as I surveyed row after row of this appalling rubbish, was what a wonderfully eccentric and unique creation the gnome was, quite old fashioned really, almost quaint – and as unappreciated as that family heirloom that's been hanging around the house for so long that no one bothers looking at it anymore. Recognized by everyone and accessible to all, gnomes have a history, they carry meaning, and they've lived in British gardens for well over a hundred years. Aren't they, in fact, something of a national treasure?

It was, after all, an Englishman who introduced the first gnome to the garden. Sir Charles Isham of Lamport Hall built his enormous ninety-foot rockery in 1847 and planted it up with dwarf conifers and alpines. Nearly twenty years would pass before he thought of animating it with gnomes, and he sent off to Germany for the porcelain dwarf-like figures,

which, until then, were confined to the drawing room. Once he had released them into the great outdoors, he was soon grouping them into scenarios, with signs and tableaux of striking miners. Isham was a spiritualist, and believed that his figures represented the gnomes of the spirit world.

The French art critic and professor of contemporary art Jean Yves Jouannais suggests in his book *Les Nains, les jardins* (*Gnomes, Gardens*) that gnomes are part of the collective unconscious. This would account for the way they sprang up spontaneously in their early incarnations in so many ancient cultures. Dwarf gods pervade the mythologies of Egypt, Greece, Persia and Turkey. The medieval folklore and fairy tales of Northern Europe which followed were alive with supernatural spirits that lived in forests, caves and wild places, variously embodied as goblins, trolls, leprechauns, elves, fairies and pygmy miners, to name but a few. Every country had its own version of these little people.

Sweden, though, is perhaps the only country to have preserved its gnome folklore in its purest and simplest form. Uncorrupted by mass production or commercialism, the Swedish gnome has survived, virtually unaltered over hundreds of years, as a much-loved figure in Sweden's cultural heritage. They call him the *tomte*. A diminutive chap with a long white or grey beard and a pointed red cap, he was the benevolent spirit that watched over the farm. He lived in the stable or barn, helped with the chores and looked after the animals, with which he had a particular affinity as he could talk to them. The *tomte* brought luck to the farmer, but would only stay if the farmer was kind to his animals, his family, and remembered, every Christmas Eve, to put out a bowl of porridge for him to eat. As the farms disappeared, the *tomte* moved into the house, where he lived under the floorboards. In the 1870s, this legend was revived by the Swedish artist Jenny Nystrom, who popularized it with her charming illustrations in children's books, magazines and greeting cards, often depicting the *tomte* in traditional Swedish Christmas scenes. This reinforced his association with Christmas and it is now customary to set the *tomte* out in the snow with his lantern. For the rest of the year he lives in the garden, a symbol of luck. With few exceptions, there is only one *tomte* to each garden, as the Swedes don't seem tempted to collect them in quantity. They are individually crafted, produced in small cottage industries or imported from Europe.

It is a huge leap from the simple and secure lives led by gnomes in unspoiled Nordic forests and lakes to the controversy and complexity of gnome gardens in Britain. Gnomes are a potent symbol and I suspect that this is why they became popular in the no-man's-land of the newly created suburbias of the twentieth century. Cut adrift from both city and countryside, a garden gnome, set out on the concrete doorstep or on the bare lawn, was a way of dropping anchor. I wonder how many of the members of the various gnome liberation groups weren't themselves brought up in suburbia, and identify with what they call 'gnomes in captivity'. Why else would they care so much? The anthropologist Professor Patrick Boumard of the University of Rennes has held a three-day seminar and written a dissertation on the relationship between the French and their gnomes. In it, he has described the garden gnome as a totem of the times we live in and fraught with all sorts of symbolism – economic, cultural and emotional.

While gnomes are now being analysed by social scientists, appropriated by the advertising industry and ridiculed by the media, they

are championed by a devoted band of followers whose simple pleasure it is to gather them into their gardens. Since the publication of Wil Huygen's book *Gnomes*, with illustrations by Rien Poortvliet, in 1976, and the creation of the Gnome Reserve in Devon in 1979, gnomes have quietly acquired a cult following. Huygen reinvented the folklore of the gnomes and Poortvliet's illustrations were so wonderful that gnomes have been made from them. The Gnome Reserve has become a place of pilgrimage, and is regarded by gnome collectors as their spiritual home. Over a thousand of them are spread out under a canopy of beech trees, and spill out into the wildflower garden. It was founded by the landscape artist Ann Atkin, inspired by the beliefs in the healing powers of creativity and nature espoused by her husband, the artist Ron Atkin. For her, the gnome is a personification of the creative imagination,

inseparable from nature, and something of a personal muse. He is as ancient as he is young, his pyramid-shaped hat pointing to the heavens even as his feet are firmly rooted on the ground. He connects heaven with earth and thus reflects the ecological interdependence of all life on the planet. However, this is a personal philosophy and you will not find these thoughts spelled out at the Reserve. 'Gnomes can be anything you want them to be,' she says, 'and people see them differently.' She leaves the gnomes to cast their spell on your subconscious. Most of the gnomes were made by her son Richard, and his wife Meg looks after the 250 species of wild flowers, which are an important part of the ethos of the Reserve. Their two children, Mark and Joe, help their parents carry the gnomes in and out of hibernation every year.

Gnomes, once openly placed in the front garden with pride and trust have now, thanks to pranksters and vandals, been removed to the safety of the house and back garden. This has made gnome gardens harder to find, and many have vanished. So it was with amazement that I came across a long line-up of gnomes on a wall beside a busy dual carriageway in Cornwall. It is the oldest gnome garden in this book and belongs to a couple in their eighties. The gnomes were made by their sons, who are now in their sixties, when they were children and sold to earn extra pocket money. Dozens of them sat there quite happily until one day they all vanished overnight, and were later found dumped and smashed in a nearby field. Undeterred, the couple bravely returned what remained of the gnomes to the garden, where some of them now sit on the wall, protected by barbed wire.

A great expert and collector of outsider art, Maggie M was given a stone gnome about fifteen years ago, which she painted herself. It was

subsequently stolen from her front garden. 'The theft of my favourite gnome drove me on to start collecting more and, like any collection, it seemed to form its own impetus, with gnomes appearing from nowhere, in unexpected places, as if they were waiting for me. I found gnomes abandoned, gnomes in Swiss hypermarkets and Belgian roadside stalls. Some American friends gave me a vivid green light-up gnome, miniature gnomes were found in Austria, giant gnomes from Germany. I don't like to spend a lot of money on them, my favourites are from thrift shops and kitsch Asian household stores.' Most of the collection has been gathered into a grotto under an old forsythia, where she can see them when she's doing the washing up. The rest live on the lawn under a giant toadstool she found in a junk shop. 'I love the gnomes' sense of community,' she says, 'the feeling that they are a little civilization all of their own. They create their own territory as they congregate outside my kitchen window. They bring amusement and joy and make everyone smile. They are a force for good in the world.'

The collection of gnomes at St Joseph's Hospice in Hackney was started by Sister Mary Wynne many years ago, when she made gnomes from rubber moulds with the patients in the day hospice. They live at the bottom of the garden, in a peaceful oasis, shielded from traffic behind the hospice and serenaded by a trickling waterfall. The gnomes, I am told by head gardener Jocelyn Armitage, come and go and don't always stay where they're put. 'New ones arrive every year. Sometimes they just appear and sometimes people bring them personally and ask if we could keep them as a sort of memorial to a deceased relative. A few gnomes also move on. Some are never seen again. One was missing for about a year but he returned after the run of his stage show, *A Gnome*

from Home at Hoxton Hall.' The gnomes, she says, 'are a talking point, and a diversion from more serious matters.' And although they harbour snails under their hollow feet, spoil her borders with their gaudy colours, and seem to taunt her with their mocking expressions as she weeds, they have, she says, 'an understanding. We are both in the business of trying to lift the spirits of the dying. They do their thing, I do mine.' Of all the benches that are dotted around the hospice gardens, the ones most frequented are the two that overlook the gnomes. Staff and patients like sitting there, as do visitors of all ages. 'The children love the gnomes because, when they come here, it's a sad time for them,' said one of the nurses.

Gnomes are optimists, they breathe contentment. 'They incarnate, because of their adorable earthiness of spirit, the myth of happiness,' writes Jouannais. The late David Pullen created his own vision of utopia in his back garden over a period of thirty-five years. It started quite by accident, when he and his wife Maggie fell in love with a fat little gnome in a garden centre because it resembled their chubby three-year-old son. From that moment, regular weekend excursions to the gnome manufacturers in Sheerness assured a car boot groaning with the weight of concrete gnomes on their return. Maggie was in charge of painting them, but David planned the garden. In it, he realized his nostalgic dream of an idyllic Sunday afternoon in a rural English village that harked back to a time when villages were real communities. Everyone was out of the house, relaxing in their gardens, fishing and generally milling about. Some had come out to watch the Salvation Army band playing on the green, and the cricketers were on the pitch. Only the cricketers were real men, but almost everyone else was a gnome. The red Wendy houses

were built for his grandchildren. 'David was a serious man, a tidy man,' recalls Maggie. 'He was an engineer and took life seriously. But when he came home, he switched off from the real world when he stepped into the fantasy world of his garden. Every gnome had its place, its personality and a purpose. It all had to make sense, and it all had to mean something. His family never had a lot of money when he was growing up and there were a lot of things he couldn't have as a child, and his garden was a bit of that lost childhood being recaptured. He wanted his children to have what he hadn't had and what they would like.' David died of cancer three years ago, and his last request was that David Bowie's *The Laughing Gnome* be played at his funeral. 'When everyone came out of the church,' says Maggie, 'they all had smiles on their faces.'

And then there is Ron, who really is a gnome. He already had a few gnomes when, depressed by the end of his marriage, he went to see his doctor. The doctor told him to get a hobby, and that this would be better than any pills he could prescribe. So he started collecting gnomes, which he cemented down in his front garden. To raise charity money for his working men's club, he grew a beard. The local children who passed by his house on their way to school caught sight of him and said, 'You look like a gnome, you should dress like one as well.' Their mothers got together and made him an outfit. Now retired, he devotes his time to raising money for the NSPCC. He has charity boxes with his picture on in various shops in town and twice a week, he puts on his gnome outfit and trundles his shopping trolley around town, collecting money for the charity. He tells the children stories about gnomes on charity picnics and at his stall on the market square. He

wants to get them away from television and computer games, which, he says, are all about monsters killing each other. 'The reason why you don't see gnomes,' he tells them, 'is that gnomes come alive at night and look after the plants and animals. When people go into their garden at night and talk to their plants, it's the gnomes underneath they're really talking to.' A couple of years ago, Selfridges recreated part of his house and back garden for one of their Christmas windows. The crowds that gathered round to view the 100 gnomes on display were, at one point, such an obstruction on Oxford Street that the police had to move them on.

Although every gnome garden has a different story, they are all, in a way, saying the same thing. And no one has captured their atmosphere more eloquently then Ben Okri, in his novel *In Arcadia*.

> There were gnomes all over the garden, giving the place a jovial feel. It was as if nature was smiling, enjoying a joke under the sun, always laughing, always aware of the essential humour of all living things. The gnomes seemed to be laughing at all the stress, all fretting, all inflation of human things to levels of greater importance than they truly deserved.

Gnomes are all about how you perceive them, and the more you look, the more you see.

Vivian Russell

TO THE GNOMES →

ADMISSION - FROM THE HOUSE - ALSO
GNOME HATS - DO ALL BORROW ONE TO BE
APPROPRIATELY DRESSED TO VISIT THE
GNOMES (LOANED FREE OF CHARGE - GOOD FOR PHOTOS!)

PLEASE KEEP
TO THE PATH

YOU ARE HERE

49

THIS WATERFALL
HAS BEEN DONATED
WITH GREAT PLEASURE
TO ST. JOSEPH'S HOSPICE BY:
JOSEPH & ZELDA BARNETT
of Leytonstone, London E. 11.
FOUNDERS of LEYTONIA RADIO

WARNING
KEEP YOUNG CHILDREN
IN HAND
SHALLOW WATER

PICTURE CREDITS

Half title The Gnome Reserve, Devon
Title A Rien Poortvliet gnome, Christina V's garden, Norrkoping, Sweden
4 The Gnome Reserve, Devon
6 A Jenny Nystrom Christmas card, 1890s
7 Ingrid's 1950s gnomes, Jonkoping, Sweden
8 Wildflower garden, the Gnome Reserve, Devon
9 Suburban garden, Normandy, France
10 Maggie M's kitchen window, near Watford (above); a member of David Pullen's Salvation Army band, north London (below)
12 Ron the Gnome (above); Ron's shopping trolley with gnomes and NSPCC charity box on board (below)
13 The entrance to the Gnome Reserve woodland, Devon
14–15 Christina V's garden, Norrkoping, Sweden
16–17 David Pullen's garden, north London
18–19 Niall and Alistair's kitchen garden mascot, Fintry, Scotland
20–21 The Gnome Reserve, Devon
22–23 Gnomes made by Ann Atkin, the Gnome Reserve, Devon
24–25 Maggie M's grotto, near Watford

26 Ron the Gnome's garden, Lincolnshire
27 The Gnome Reserve, Devon
28–29 The Gnome Reserve, Devon
30–31 Wildflower garden, the Gnome Reserve, Devon
32 Ulf's gnomes, Norrkoping, Sweden
33 Dittmar and Monica's gnome, Sodra Finno, Sweden
34–35 Maggie M's toadstool lawn, near Watford
36–37 My gnome garden, Lake District
38–39 St Joseph's Hospice, Hackney (left and right); the Gnome Reserve, Devon (middle)
40–41 Mrs Copp's garden, Dorset
42 David Pullen's garden, north London
43 St Joseph's Hospice, Hackney (left); David Pullen's garden, north London (right)
44–45 Mr and Mrs Bassett's garden, Cornwall
46–47 Ron the Gnome's garden, Lincolnshire
48–49 Mr and Mrs Bassett's garden, Cornwall
50 Eva-Lotta and Kurt-Evert's garden, Vetlanda, Sweden
51 Siggge's gnome, Norrkoping, Sweden

52–53 The garden of Peter R, a retired joiner, Loch Ness, Scotland
54–55 The Gnome Reserve, Devon
56–57 The Gnome Reserve, Devon
58 Mr and Mrs Bassett's garden, Cornwall (left); The Gnome Reserve, Devon (right)
59 Gullan's garden, Jonkoping, Sweden (left); Ron the Gnome's garden, Lincolnshire (right)
60 John and Pamela L's garden, near Troon, Scotland
61 The Gnome Reserve, Devon
62–63 St Joseph's Hospice, Hackney
64–65 Norrkoping, Sweden
66 The Gnome Reserve, Devon (left); David Pullen's garden, north London (right)
67 David Pullen's garden, north London
68 Ron the Gnome's garden, Lincolnshire
69 The Gnome Reserve, Devon
70–71 Ron the Gnome's garden, Lincolnshire
72 Ron the Gnome's garden Lincolnshire (left); St Joseph's Hospice, Hackney (right)
73 The Gnome Reserve, Devon
74–75 The Gnome Reserve, Devon (left and right); Mr and Mrs Bassett's garden, Cornwall (middle)

76–77 St Joseph's Hospice, Hackney
78 Mr and Mrs Bassett's back door, Cornwall
79 Ron the Gnome's window sill, Lincolnshire
80 Robert and Jane G's garden, Kirkcudbright, Scotland
81 Ron the Gnome's garden, Lincolnshire
82–83 The Gnome Reserve, Devon
84–85 John and Pamela L's garden, near Troon, Scotland
86 John and Pamela L's garden, near Troon, Scotland
87 Mr and Mrs Bassett's garden, Cornwall
88–89 The Gnome Reserve, Devon (left and middle); Mrs Copp's garden, Dorset (right)
90–91 David Pullen's garden, north London
92 Harry's garden, Lammhult, Sweden
93 Ladies in the wildflower garden, the Gnome Reserve, Devon
94–95 Robert and Jane G's garden, Kirkcudbright, Scotland
96 Mrs Copp's garden, Dorset
97 Christer and Christina's 1950s Italian gnomes, Jonkoping, Sweden
98 Ulf's gnome, Norrkoping, Sweden

ACKNOWLEDGMENTS

This book is dedicated to Ann Atkin, founder of the Gnome Reserve, in appreciation of all the joy she has given to so many visitors.

I would like to thank everyone whose gnomes appear in this book for welcoming me into their gardens, and am only sorry, that in order to protect them from vandals, I can't reveal their precise locations. However, a huge thank you goes to Penelope Hobhouse, who told me about Mrs Copp's garden, and also to Sr Angela and Catherine Clear at St Joseph's Hospice. I am particularly grateful to Jeppe Wikstrom for his kind invitation to photograph the gnomes in Sweden, and to his assistants, Johanna Smolander and Erika Berggren, who organized my trip so efficiently that gnomes materialised, as if by magic. I wouldn't have found any of them were it not for fellow photographer Marcus Eriksson, who chauffeured me on a madcap journey through some three hundred miles of Swedish countryside, finding places so remote they weren't even on the car's satellite navigation map. Thank you to Eva Londos, who spent a day taking us round to meet and photograph her tomte friends in Jonkoping, and to Mr and Mrs Soderwall of the Strand Hotel, Norrkoping, who presented me with a very amusing tomte as a souvenir of my stay.

I am indebted to the whole team at Frances Lincoln, without whom there would be no book: Anne Fraser, who shared my sense of fun in embarking on this project, publisher John Nicoll, who indulged us, my wonderful and inspired designers, Caroline Clark and Becky Clarke, Sue Gladstone, Michael Brunström, and the whole production team, working away behind the scenes. And finally, thank you to all those people who have, over many years, created all the gnomes that appear in this book. What a delightful cast of characters has emerged from their imaginations.

Frances Lincoln Ltd
4 Torriano Mews
Torriano Avenue
London NW5 2RZ
www.franceslincoln.com

A catalogue record for this book is available from the
British Library.

ISBN 0 7112 2325 4

Printed and bound in China
by Kwong Fat Offset Printing Co. Ltd

9 8 7 6 5 4 3 2